Idaho in Pictures and Poetry

A Collection of Idaho Inspired Poems

Eloise Kraemer

Haumea Publishing Company

Idaho in Pictures and Poetry

Haumea Publishing Company

First Edition

All rights reserved

Copyright pending@2018 by Eloise Kraemer

Printed by CreateSpace, Charleston, S.C., USA

ISBN: 13:978-0-578-41960-2

Some Things Are Clearer in the Dark....

This book is dedicated to the families of Idaho, past and present. We are all a part of what Idaho is today.

Do We Dream to Create or Create to Dream?

SUNSET IN WINTER

Of all the scenes that fill the world,

a sunset is the best.

Fluffy clouds of pink and orange upon a golden crest.

Trees along the skyline, bright, set out by golden glow.

Stand as soldiers before a fight, above the jeweled snow.

Then, just before the sun goes down, and the black of night is rolled.

A sharp crack on the ice does sound, to bid farewell, the day is old.

Idaho Sunset on Water

By Cataldo, Idaho

Idaho Winter Sunset

THE MINER
(A Tribute to Miners of Idaho, past and present)

His 'hard boiled' hat atop his head,

was painted a dull and rusty red.

His face was dusty, tired and thin.

His hand was rested 'neath his chin.

His clothes were grimy, dark and damp.

At his side lay a tin pail and carbide lamp.

His pick and shovel lay near his feet.

His boots looked muddy, worn, and beat.

Such is a miner when day's work is done.

He trundles home, his wages won.

Galena Mine, Lake Gulch, Wallace, ID

Primarily a silver, zinc and lead mine

Still Operational – Employs approximately 157

Old Mine Tunnel – Circa- 1920s

In the Idaho Panhandle, the 'Silver Valley', (consisting of the towns Cataldo, Kingston, Pinehurst, Murray, Prichard, Kellogg, Smelterville, Osburn, Wallace and Mullan), still mines gold, lead, silver zinc, antimony, tungsten, bismuth, and trace amounts of other minerals. The primary metals are silver, zinc, and lead. During the 1970s, it is said that nearly half the nation's silver production came from the 'Silver Valley' of Northern Idaho.

The Boise Basin gold rush of the 1860s was one of the biggest in American history. In 1864, Idaho City, in the center of Boise Basin, had a population of 7,000, making it (at that time) the largest city in the Northwest. It was actually bigger than Portland in population.

Mining also takes place, today, in Custer, Camas and Blaine counties. They mine galena, sphalerite, chalcopyrite, and **tetrahedrite.**

Silver City served as the county seat of Owyhee County from 1867 to 1934. In the 1880s, Silver City, Idaho had a population of about 2,500 and was a busy gold and silver mining town. Silver City is now a ghost town, and serves as a popular tourist destination.

According to the "Mining in Idaho" website; the greater share of Idaho's phosphate *mining is done in eastern* Idaho *around Soda Springs. Phosphate reserves in* Idaho are *in Bear Lake, Bingham, Bonneville, and Caribou counties. It was noted that in 1974, phosphate was* Idaho's *second leading mineral and close to silver in value at that time.*

Another little known mineral mined in Idaho from the early 1900's through the late 1930s, was coal. The coal mine was located in the Teton Mountains, near Sam,

Idaho, just west of Driggs, Idaho. Sam, Idaho is now a ghost town.

Henry F. Samuels, a lawyer, one of the original partners in the Hercules Mining Company, Wallace, Idaho, invested in the coal mine in the 1920's. He was instrumental in keeping a spur of the Oregon Shortline Railroad active for hauling out the ore through the late 1930's. Sam, Idaho was named for H.F. Samuels, as was Samuels, Idaho above Sandpoint.

It might be also noted that H.F. Samuels is considered the "father of the zinc industry in Idaho". He developed a more effective process for removing zinc from lead.

An Indian Summer Eve

Silent, windless and warm is the air.

Colored brightly are the leaves.

No other time can quite compare,

to an Indian summer eve.

One by one, the leaves do fall,

on grasses, golden brown.

Into ponds, and streams that lull,

through meadows filled with thistle down.

A frog, his song to the world, now sings.

Geese to the south take flight.

In the wind, a song of peacefulness rings,

as a full moon rises, and the sun bids

good-night.

Fall Colors, Algoma, Idaho

The Bitterroots of the Rockies

High in the Bitterroot Mountains,

in forests, thick and green,

Streams make nature's fountains,

of burbling water, fresh and clean.

Here mosses carpet woodland trails,

and wild flower gardens grow.

A wolf pack sounds its eerie wails,

as pine trees waver to and fro.

White tailed deer with dappled fawns,

in an alpine meadow play,

Cottontails, on forest lawns,

frolic, at the close of day.

Songbirds send music, sweet,

throughout the woodland trees.

Black bear lifts up its nose to greet,

a passing forest breeze.

The sun shines its sparkling rays,

on grasses, green to golden brown.

And every hill, till sunset, stays,

decked with a multi-colored crown.

Here, only nature paints the scene,

as she cuts, and shapes and hews.

Her smallest wish exceeds man's greatest dream,

her work disdained by few.

A Mountain Holiday

Nature is decorating for the Holidays!

It's dressing in ice and in snow.

The light shining down from the heavens,

sets the whole world aglow!

Trees stand like marching soldiers,

white coats on troops of blue-gray.

The winds chase clouds on a darkening sky,

to curtain the end of the day.

Another day closer to celebrating!

Closer to a bright New Year!

A bird sends a song through the darkness, brimming with holiday cheer!

Happy Holidays to all creatures.

Good health to you all.

May your cities prosper, and your forests grow tall.

Here's to all of nature,

To all living things on our earth!

May we all learn to live together,

and to cherish each other's worth!

Snowshoeing Near Rose Lake, Idaho

Moose Munch

The Trail of the Coeur d' Alene's, lies on a railroad bed.

I decided to walk on the trail, but, rode my bike instead.

The birds were singing.

The breezes were soft, not a cloud in the sky.

I ventured off the trail, set down my bike, then, waded in the creek – I don't know why.

I head a rustle and a thump by an old chokecherry tree...

Next, I heard a crunch, and a munch, drawing closer to me.

I went for my bike, set beside the Coeur d'Alene Trail.

I was just about to climb under the middle bridge rail,

when, out of the bushes stepped a raggedy young moose.

He looked too young to be alone, on the loose.

Just as the thought appeared in my mind,

'Papa Moose' came up on me from behind.

His head went down, as she showed me his rack,

I grabbed my bike and shouldered my pack.

He snorted, and then he blew.

That's when I stumbled and lost my shoe.

I didn't say good-by and I didn't look back.

As I pedaled like mad, down the railroad bed track.

A Mountain for Heartaches

Past year's bright memories shine,

like jewels on the snow,

while heartaches are softened,

by a silent white blanket on the forests below.

A lonely osprey soars above, soft wings whoosh, quite near.

The morning light casts a hint of a rainbow.

An icicle drips a tear.

The trees move in harmony with nature's soft breeze.

A new day, a new year, and heartaches will ease.

Smith's Ferry, ID

An Idaho Girl Goes to Nevada

(Tribute to my time in the wild deserts of Nevada)

When I was young, and played in the mountains of Idaho, I dreamed of owning a camel…..

Now, I live in the desert and build stone walls.

I dream of mountains, pine trees, waterfalls….

And think of love, long lost in that place….

While the hot wind and sun, each day I must face.

But, even as I mourn the loss of things dear,

The years have taught me to appreciate what is near.

While pausing to listen to the coyote's faint wails,

I marvel at an eagle – high above, where he sails.

A lizard suns himself on a stone,

while a jackrabbit peeks out of his

burrow-type home.

I wake in the morning to the sound of a dove,

and retire in the evening to hoot owls in love.

My water is pumped from under the ground.

Waterfalls are built, but they make the same sound.

Each tree, I have planted, and watered to grow.

When the wind blows, they rustle...then, I know....

A little of everything is part of another.

A little of each is kin to the other.

It matters not where you are, if, in all you do,

you look for that you love in the things near to you.

Camels near Virginia City, NV

The Fawn

The late autumn leaves rustled, and up popped the head of a half grown fawn.

His mother and he had been running till early dawn.

Now it was time to run again,

away from the hunters, (strange stick-carrying men).

They had just time to get a drink and a bite of grass before a snapping stick...

gave a warning, "Run! Run, Quick!"

A squirrel chatters from a nearby tree, "Now! Be on your way!"

This is the price that the hunted pay!

They ran for hours and hours it seemed, before they came to rest in a quiet ravine.

But, even here, danger lurked.

The hunter's stick cracked, his mother suddenly jerked.

She fell to the ground, with a sigh.

There, cold as a stone would she lie.

Little snowflakes began to drift down upon her nose.

The fawn knew he couldn't stay. He had to go!

The hunters were coming! He saw this!

He nuzzled his mother good-by with one last, little fawn kiss.

"Good-by Mother, I run alone now, as I flee for my life."

Ahead of him lies unknown strife.

He uttered one – last – sad little bleat….

And ran as he heard the hunter's scurrying feet.

Young Whitetail, Pend' Oreille, ID

Whitetail Doe, Pinehurst, Idaho

GOLD

Golden light shines golden rays, on golden grasses dried from summer days.

Strips of golden sunlight beam, on golden leaves, on a golden stream.

Soaring bird on a golden wing, a golden voice, with which to sing.

Golden sunset upon the peaks, from a golden world, the bright light seeps.

Fall Colors on Pend' Oreille River by Oldtown, Idaho

(After leaving Pend' Oreille Lake, the river flows north into Canada)

THE HITCHHIKER ON SH-3

I chanced upon a hitchhiker along state highway 3.

He looked a rumpled, worn and tired state, to me.

Sometimes, things make you pause a bit, to appreciate where you're at….

I thought of this, as the wind blew off his battered old fishing hat.

The shoes he wore were next to none,

his face was withered by the sun.

His pants were drab, torn and patched,

his wrinkled shirt all but matched.

His ragged beard was gray and white,

but those eyes! So merry! So blue! So bright!

As though he lived a life of ease,

with all his needs and wants appeased.

State Highway-3, Cataldo, Idaho

Bridges

Joining one side to the other is a marvelous engineering feat,

Each one has a different look and is called a bridge when it's complete.

Connecting places over, under, around and through,

That's what man makes bridges do.

There are bridges over water, and bridges over land.

There are bridges over bridges and bridges over dams.

There are bridges that swing and bridges that float.

I've seen bridges that can turn into a boat!

We have bridges that raise, open and close.

We even have a bridge on top of our nose!

What would we do without bridges to view or cross?

The separation would be quite a loss.

Veteran's Memorial Centennial Bridge
Bennett Bay on I-90, Coeur d'Alene, ID – 1990

Completed Veteran's Memorial Centennial Bridge

Bennett Bay, Coeur d'Alene, Idaho I-90

It was completed 1991. It took $20 million to complete.

It is a segmental concrete box girder bridge, 1730 feet long and 70 feet wide. It sits 300 feet above the valley floor.

Rainbow Bridge – State Highway 55 by Smith's Ferry, Idaho

Sandpoint, Idaho – Train Bridge Crossing Lake Pend' Oreille

Lake Pend' Oreille has a maximum depth of 1,150 feet, and is the fifth deepest lake in the United States.

Lake Pend' Oreille actually boasts an inland naval submarine base at Bayview, Idaho.

Idaho Cottontails

In amongst the pine trees, rustling with the wind,

Play the little cottontails with their next of kin.

Underneath the toadstools, spotted brown and white,

Hide the little cottontails, when in danger, they take flight.

Whiskers twitching, noses wiggling, tails of powder-puff,

Two ears upon a cottontail just like a furry tuff.

Wriggling in and out of bushes, hiding by the streams,

playing drop the leaf and chestnuts, just like children, it would seem.

Until the sun sets on the peaks, and Mother summons with thumps of feet.

Then, all the cottontails scamper home, to their waiting mom,

to fall asleep beneath the stars, to wait until the dawn.

Young Rabbit on His First Outing

Idaho Mountain Meadow

Of Idaho's Statehouse Statues

If those statues of stone could speak, I wonder what they'd say.

Of wars and loves and lives of men, who lived within their day?

Of the man that carved that stony face, for them, eternity.

They watch us come and go, as tides upon the sea.

Yet, as they stand,

as all alone,

these eternal statues, carved

of stone,

we know not what secrets they behold,

In silent eyes, so warm,

Yet, so distant,

so cold.

Gilded Statue of George Washington

Boise, Idaho Statehouse

Reflection of the State Capitol, Boise, Idaho

An Idaho Thanksgiving

Thank you for sun and sky.

Thank you, too, for birds that fly.

Thank you for many happy days, and for parents to guide us in our ways.

Thank you for the food we eat.

Also, for the friends we meet.

Thanks for someone there to understand, when, at times, we need a helping hand.

Thank you for health and warmth and laughter.

And for dreams we have worth searching after.

Thank you for flowers, and trees….

Yes, thank you for all of these.

Thank you could be listed, more, and then more.

To give thanks is what we made Thanksgiving for!

Thanksgiving Eve by Lake Coeur d'Alene

Idaho Turkey Dinner

Shadows

Fleeting shadows in the night, under stars and yellow moon light. Dark as death on the frozen ground, Erie shapes without a sound.

Shadows by Old Mission, Cataldo, ID

In Memory of Memee

At night, when the moon shines bright,

and the frogs and the crickets sing,

an owl cries out through the cloudless night,

and tearful memories bring.

She was small and dainty, eyes of blue,

a ball of soft grey fur.

No sound was quite as nice as my kitten's loving purr.

When I'd pause from chores a bit,

in the middle of the day,

my kitten would tell in little mews.......

her stories, in her own sweet way.

She would tell of how her day had passed.

And how she nearly caught, a butterfly, and how she scared the ducks,

when she knew she hadn't 'ought.

And with the other cats,

she'd play,

just like children,

one might say,

Games like –

'Who's the Scaredy Cat?'

and, 'Who Can Catch

the Biggest Rat?'

In the evening,

like a scurrying ghost,

the time of day

she loved the most, into the

fields, she would fly,

chasing moonbeams,

back to the sky.

Then, one day, she wasn't there,

to greet me with the sun.

And, still, my kitten wasn't there when,

yet the day was done.

The next day, I found her,

high on a lofty hill.

The owl had taken my Memee,

He left her there, His kill.

Memee, an Idaho Kitten That Was

What is Life in Idaho?

What is Idaho life to me?

Maybe it's the first spring blossom on a tree.

Maybe it's a sunny meadow, or a sparkling brook, a joyful laugh, a wistful look?

Maybe….crisp leaves of gold, silver, orange or red,

or, quiet woodland paths, that I love to tread.

Maybe it is….flaming sunsets on winter snows,

a frosty window or a cold nose!

I see life in cloudy skies and thunder showers,

in ringing bells in high church towers…..

Life is a newborn foal, a hatching chick….

or children by a campfire, toasting marshmallows on a willow stick….

Life is laughter, life is sad.

Life sees the good and life sees the bad.

But most of all, life is enduring hope, which makes it worth climbing the steepest slope.

Snowshoeing by Chain Lakes, North Idaho

The Logger

I heard a crack….I heard a boom!

The jarring shook my cabin room.

A large machine began to roar, as the pounding began upon my door.

I opened the door to a red flannel shirt that was set off by suspenders, some grease and some dirt.

His jeans were worn, his boots were scuffed.

His pocket bulged with a can of snuff.

A man as tall as a sapling tree,

announced his entry, as he smiled at me.

He wanted to let me know, so as not to scare,

the reason his men and machines were there.

My neighbor had decided to cut his trees that day,

just like a farmer cuts his hay.

His swather, though, was mighty large.

It was more the size of a landlocked barge.

He needed no blade, axe or saw, just one big excavator, with a mighty jaw.

It nudged the tree with a tap or two.

On the third nudge, it knew what to do.

The tree gave up, roots and all.

Another... boom! I watched it fall.

A logger's job is never easy, safe or done.

Although, the look on his face makes me think it might just sometimes be fun.

Throughout Idaho's history, logging has been an important industry.

At the turn of the twentieth century, it was said that forest resources had a higher economic benefit to the state of Idaho than mining.

Whiteman Lumber, Established 1928
5 Generations have worked here

The Union Pacific Freight

I still remember the sound of the train, as it pulled away from the loading dock.

It hitched the cars with a 'clunkity-clunkclunk' and ended with a knock-knockknock.

With hitched up cars, the train gave a 'toot' 'toot toot',

As if anyone really gave a hoot!

It moved forward, loaded with ore containing silver, iron, bismuth, antimony, lead and zinc.

After picking up more cars it would head to the smelter, in Kellogg, back then, I think.

It took a bit before the train would gain full speed.

It would toot a few more loud blasts (in front of our house) for autos to heed.

For it was crossing a road with no signal arm.

Now, that could be more than a little cause for alarm!

Especially, if you weren't quite awake,

And it happened to be the road you had to take.

Once in motion, and loaded with ore, the train was one mighty plow.

It couldn't stop without some time, the brakes just didn't know how!

Now, to get to the highway, you had to stop where the tracks were laid.

The loaded train needed speed to climb the coming steeper grade.

Early one morning, as the train started out, loaded with his ore,

Our neighbor, short on coffee, decided to pause on the track and immediately began to snore.

As we crossed our bridge, on our way to school, the train began tooting and ringing its bell.

The impending crash was plain to see as we all ran, waving, shouting as well.

Brakes were squealing, our heads were reeling, when train hit the neighbor's red truck.

We watched in horror and hoped the driver had enough time to jump or to duck!

The train finally stopped, the truck was now scrunched.

The fate of our neighbor, we hadn't a hunch.

Happily, he had only a few bruises and a bad dream to boot.

But, the next time he woke when he heard a train toot!

Northern Pacific Train Depot, Wallace, ID

It was constructed in 1901. It is now a Train Museum

The last ore train (Union Pacific) ran in Wallace in 1994.

An Idaho Farmer

An Idaho farmer never gets in any hurry,

There's no sense in that, you know.

The job is the same every day, no

matter sun, rain, wind or snow.

You can count on him to be there, the

same time every day.

He hardly needs a clock for time,

he'd probably lose it anyway!

He's up with the chickens,

because, chickens like to be fed,

He's out again at dark with the cows,

because, cows like to be put to bed.

The crops need to be watered, or the crops need to be sowed.

The crops need to be picked or the crops need to be mowed.

The land needs to be leveled, or the land needs to be plowed.

The land needs to be fenced, or fertilized, and the machinery can't be too loud.

The story of a farmer is as old as this land,

For farm raised products, there's still high demand.

Potatoes and onions, corn, wheat and soy,

rape seeds and sugar beets, alfalfa….pure joy!

Some farmers like to raise,

cattle and hogs,

Some would rather have sheep,

guarded by sheep dogs,

Some even farm trees,

fruit orchard, or pine

They have horse farms, fish farms, alligator farms, even honeybee farms are fine.

Farmers are still needed,

in our great State of Idaho.

With a country to feed,

we will always need farmers to grow.

Idaho Farmer, Boise, Idaho

Old Barn near Cataldo, Idaho

4X4 Stables

4X4 Stables once stood where Northgate Shopping Center, State Street and Gary Lane now stands. It was torn down in the '80s to make room for progress.

Farmer Plowing His Field

On The Palouse Between Moscow

and Lewiston, ID

Grain grown from this area is hauled from here to the Clearwater River that runs through Lewiston, ID to be barged out to the Pacific coast to be shipped to different points worldwide. Lumber and other agricultural products are also shipped. Lewiston is Idaho's only inland sea port.

NOTE: The Clearwater joins the Snake River between Lewiston, ID and Clarkston, WA., which then empties into the Columbia River at the Tri-Cities in Washington, and flows to the Pacific Ocean.

Idaho Mustang

I was riding alone one winter night,

Under the stars and yellow moon light,

When out he shot like a shooting star,

He flew over the fence with a six foot bar.

His coat was like cream on the new fallen snow,

His mane, spun silver, set the heavens aglow.

His nostrils were flaring like the devil's fire,

He had speed and stamina like he'd never tire.

His hoofs made sparks on the hard rock ground.

His echoing neigh was an eerie sound.

His eyes were glowing in the pale moon light,

With a ghostly spirit – to the last, he'd fight!

All that night, for him I sought,

But the wild, its lessons well, to him, had taught.

Sometimes when the moon and the stars in the skies,

Shine down on the earth where the cold snow lies,

If I look above on the towering cliffs,

Where the fog rolls in spiral mists,

Wild as the wilderness, free as the wind,

There stands a golden mustang, untouched by all men.

Mustangs Roaming

Idaho Mustangs can be found in six areas of Idaho:

Black Mountain, Hard Trigger and Sands Basin in the Owyhee Mountains

The Challis area

Saylor Creek, south of Glenns Ferry

Four Mile, East of Weiser

Honker the Snow Goose

My name is Honker the Snow Goose

I was born to fly, not slog, like a moose

I honk like a horn.

I was hatched, I wasn't born.

I have feathers that are soft, white and thick.

I was hatched in a nest built of grass, feathers and sticks.

I like to paddle in the rivers and the lakes.

I love the fishes, but not necessarily snakes.

I munch on grass and corn and wheat.

I never seem to get enough to eat!

I fly to the north when the weather gets warm and spring flowers bloom,

I fly to the south when the cold wind blows and winter snows loom.

I like to spend springs in North Idaho to rest,

Then I take off for Canada to enjoy the summer and build a nest!

Snow Geese look similar to these Tundra Swans on the Chain Lakes below Rose Lake, ID. They also stop by on their way south. It is hard to tell the difference, but snow geese have black tipped wings and shorter necks.

I didn't catch any Snow Geese with my camera. I believe these are also Tundra Swans in Cataldo, ID.

Poetry in the 21st Century

Poems have been written about Christmas.

Poems have been written about time.

Poems have been written about winter.

Poems don't all seem to rhyme.

My mind is a blank.

It doesn't want to think.

Maybe I should go to the kitchen,

then, pour myself a drink.

Something soon must happen,

To change my poor muddled mind.

I just have to keep digging deeper,

To see what my imagination might find.

Oh wait! As the clock chimes four…

what is that I see heading for my door?

It's the UPS man from Amazon Prime!

Another order in…and just in time!

Maybe that's what it is …

that has my mind in a muddle,

I am buried in the computer world,

In the "Facebook" puddle!

How this century has changed… and rearranged our world!

Astounding! So many ideas, technology has thus unfurled….

Kids build roller coasters.

Then they take a ride,

while sitting in their car seat, all buckled and tied.

All kids need is your 'Iphone' and 'Minecraft', or

that's what I'm told……

Then, please, don't interrupt them,
Unless you are extremely bold!

'Legos' were built forty years ago.

Kids actually needed some skill.

Now they need motors and programs,

and you get the bill!

Relic of the Past

Scene from McCall, ID

The Dream

I thought I'd think of what to write.

Maybe a poem would help me sleep tonight.

As I thought, I fell asleep,

and dreamed I saw a thousand sheep.

The sheep were white, black, and tan.

In the middle, there stood, a golden ram.

"Come hither," said he. "Now, follow this road.

Climb these steps; look yonder, to sky,

then count my gold."

"Gold, but, where?" said I.

Gazing intently,

I searched that sky.

The ram replied, "When the stars are,

gold to you,

rich as gold,

even, the morning dew,

Then, you will see, and you will sleep,

Gently floating into the misty deep."

Idaho Sunset, Boise, Idaho

A Wish

I wish that you wake to the sound of the breaking dawn,

And sleep when you please to a brook's sweet song.

I wish that while choosing how to spend each day,

You have time to ponder what the wild geese say.

I wish that you taste a honeysuckle bright with dew,

Then, catch a fish, maybe a few!

I wish that you read to your grandchildren, walk with your husband or wife,

Enjoy the warm firelight, and drink the sweet wine of life.

Camas in Bloom

Kayaking on Rose Lake, ID

Where Do They Get Those Things?

Idahoans get their inspiration from sunrises and sunsets,

from the warm winds and the cold winter breeze.

They then mine their determination from cool mountain waters,

From lofty mountain peaks, and the stubborn roots of trees.

Revette Lake Near the Idaho/Montana Border Close to Thompson Pass

Sunset Over Chain Lakes, Cataldo, ID

Brundage Mountain, McCall, Idaho

Stubborn Tree

Pulaski Trail, Wallace, ID

Lionshead, Selkirk Range,

Boundary County, Idaho

(Highest Peak in Idaho is 7714 aka Boundary County)

Determined Tree

Pulaski Trail, Wallace, Idaho

Teton Mountains and Teton Valley, Northeast of Idaho Falls

Maidenform Peak is the highest peak at 11,138 feet.

The range borders Idaho and Wyoming. The peak is in Wyoming.

Sawtooth Mountains by Stanley, ID

Thompson Peak is the tallest peak at 10,751 feet

History is the Foundation of Our Future and Poetry is a Way to Remember the Past.

Idaho Rural Idaho Housing Complex

www.ingramcontent.com/pod-product-compliance
Lightning Source LLC
Chambersburg PA
CBHW040440190426
43202CB00034B/20